Clay-Dough Play-Dough

by Goldie Taub Chernoff

Clay-dough creations and drawings
by Margaret A. Hartelius

SCHOLASTIC BOOK SERVICES
NEW YORK • TORONTO • LONDON • AUCKLAND • SYDNEY • TOKYO

15 14 13 12 11 10 9 8 7   ISBN: 0-590-04548-2   3 4 5 6/8

Printed in the U.S.A.

Working with Clay-Dough

TO MAKE CLAY-DOUGH

You will need:
1 cup of all purpose flour
½ cup of salt
About ⅓ cup of water

- Mix the salt and flour together in a bowl.
- Add the water a little at a time. Squeeze the dough with your hands until it is smooth.
- If the clay-dough gets crumbly, wet your hands with a little water. If the dough gets too wet, sprinkle it with flour and squeeze again.
- Store the clay-dough in a plastic bag until you are ready to use it.

TO WORK WITH CLAY-DOUGH

Do ALL your modeling and drying on foil. Place the foil on a cookie sheet or pie pan. It will be easier to handle.

TO COLOR CLAY-DOUGH

There are three ways to color clay-dough:

1. You can add food coloring to the water before mixing.
2. You can add food coloring to the clay-dough after you put it in the plastic bag. Squeeze the bag until the color is mixed into the dough.
3. You can make something out of clay-dough first and color it with felt-tip markers or water colors after the object is dry.

TO DRY CLAY-DOUGH

Objects can be dried in the air, or more quickly in the oven.

Air drying:

· Place the object outdoors in the sun for a few hours, or let it dry overnight on a table or windowsill. This way of drying is good for small objects such as buttons, pendants, and pins.

Oven drying:

· Place the object in a slow, 225° oven with the door closed. Bake small, thin objects for about fifteen minutes on each side. Bake thick objects for about one hour on each side.

NOTE: Children should not light the oven without adult supervision.

PROTECTING THE FINISH

If you want the things you make to last, brush them with two or three coats of clear nail polish after they are dry. This helps the clay-dough harden and keeps the paint from coming off.

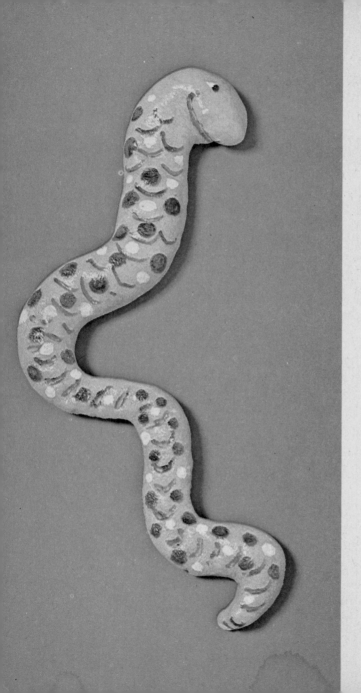

Make a Snake

· Roll a piece of clay-dough into a ball.

· Put the clay-dough on foil. Roll it out with your palms into a long rope or coil. Leave one end of the coil thick for the snake's head. Roll the other end thin for the tail.

· Press the rim of a spoon or a paper clip along the snake's back to make scales.

· Air dry or oven dry. Then color and decorate. Brush on two or three coats of clear nail polish after paint is dry.

Make Some Snails

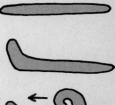

- Roll a coil.
- Turn one end of the coil up to form the snail's head.
- Roll the other end up to form the shell.
- Poke toothpick halves in the front for feelers. (They're really his eyes.)

Another way to make snails:

- Roll a short coil for the body.
- Flatten the coil and turn one end up for the head.
- Make a second coil for the shell. Roll the coil up and place it on the snail's back.

Dry in a 225° oven. Paint and decorate if you wish. Protect the finish with at least two coats of clear nail polish after the paint is dry.

Make a Bracelet or Two

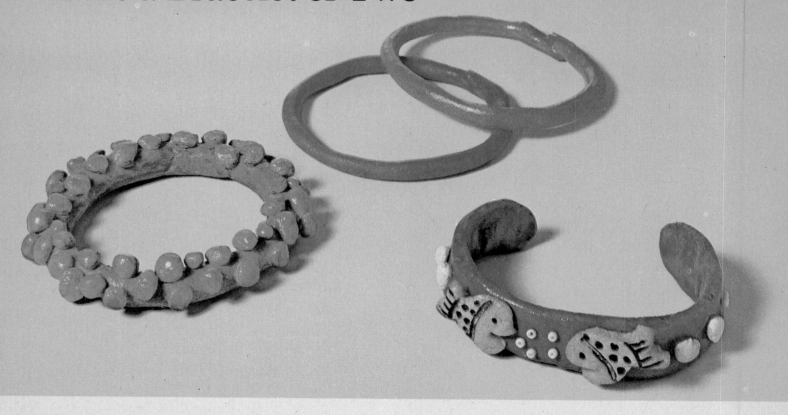

- Ask someone to help you measure your wrist with a tape measure or string. Make the measure loose so that your bracelet will slip on and off your hand.

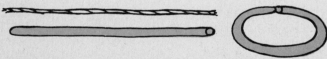

- Roll a coil the same size as the measure.

- Bring the two ends of the coil together.

- Decorate the bracelet with beads or balls of clay-dough. Dry in the air or in a 225° oven.

- Paint bracelets and put on two or three coats of clear nail polish after they are dry.

Make a Basket

- Roll a small ball of clay-dough and flatten it to make a base.

- Roll a long coil and wind it around the base.

- Continue winding and building up the sides until you have a small bowl.
- Poke two holes into opposite sides of the bowl with a pencil point.
- Dry in the oven, then decorate.

- Make a handle: Poke a ribbon or pipe cleaner through the holes.

Make a Snowman, a Clown, and Some Monsters

SNOWMAN

- Roll a large ball of clay-dough for the snowman's body.
- Then roll a small ball for the head.
- Add a small piece of clay-dough or a stick for the nose.
- Push buttons or beads into the clay for the eyes and mouth.
- Use more buttons for the snowman's jacket.
- Push in twigs for the arms.
- **Make a funny hat:** Roll a clay-dough ball and flatten it for the brim.
- Roll another ball smaller than the first. Flatten it on one side and put it on the brim like this. →

CLOWN

- Make a snowman first.
- Add a cone-shaped hat made out of clay-dough or paper.

MONSTER #1

- Push, pull, and squeeze the dough into your own kind of monster.
- Then decorate as you wish.

MONSTER #2

- Roll a large ball of clay-dough for a body.
- Then add:
    - a smaller clay-dough ball for the head;
    - two small balls for the eyes;
    - four clay-dough balls for the legs;
    - a thick coil for a tail.
- Press the rim of a spoon or a paper clip into the clay to make scales.

ALL FIGURES SHOULD BE DRIED IN A 225° OVEN.

Beads, Beads, Beads

· You can make beads in many different shapes. Roll clay-dough into small balls, egg shapes, and little coils. Or press the clay balls flat and make squares, discs, and other shapes.

· Pierce each bead with a knitting needle or a toothpick to make fairly large holes.
· Place the beads carefully on foil.
· Dry the beads in the air or in the oven.
· Color and decorate the beads. Put on at least two coats of clear nail polish to protect the finish.
· String the beads on yarn. Make a knot between each bead if you wish.

Make an Easter Egg

- Roll a ball of clay-dough into an egg shape.
- Tiny balls or coils of clay-dough can be added for decorations.
- Beads or broken jewelry can be pressed into the wet clay-dough.
- Bake in the oven at 225° for about an hour on each side. Make sure the egg is very dry.
- Let the egg cool off. Then paint it if you wish. Be sure to coat the egg with at least two coats of clear nail polish.

and an Easter Rabbit

- Roll an egg shape for the rabbit's body.
- Add a small clay ball for the nose.
- Use toothpicks for whiskers and beads for eyes.
- Dry the rabbit in the oven. Then glue on paper ears and a cotton ball for a tail.

FROG

- Roll a large ball of clay-dough.
- Flatten the bottom.
- Pinch out dough to make the mouth like this. →
- Add small balls of clay-dough for eyes.
- Pinch out dough to make feet.
- Bake. Paint when dry.

MOUSE

- Roll dough into a small egg shape for the body.
- Flatten small balls of clay-dough for the ears. Press them carefully to the head.
- Push yarn or a pipe cleaner into the clay for a tail.
- Poke eyes in with a pencil point or use beads for eyes.
- Poke toothpick halves into the mouse's back to make a porcupine.

BIRD

- Make an egg shape.
- Flatten one end like this. →
- Pull the dough out for the bill and the feet.
- Add wings. Bake, then paint.

ELEPHANT

- Roll a large ball of clay-dough.
- Flatten the bottom.
- Pull dough out for a trunk.
- Press flattened balls of clay-dough to the head for ears.
- Poke a piece of string into the clay-dough for a tail.
- Bake. Paint on feet and eyes.

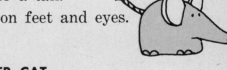

TIGER CAT

- Make an egg shape for the body.
- Then add:
  - a ball of clay-dough for the head;
  - two small balls for ears;
  - two larger balls for the cat's front paws;
  - a coil for a tail.
- Bake. Then paint on face and stripes.

DRY ANIMALS IN A 225° OVEN. REMEMBER TO COVER THE ANIMALS WITH AT LEAST TWO COATS OF CLEAR NAIL POLISH.

Make Some Tiles and Puzzles

TILES

- Roll clay-dough first with a jar or rolling pin until you have a slab about ¼ inch thick.
- Place a small box, a lid, a square of cardboard or a dish on top of the slab.

- Cut around the shape with a nail file or butter knife.
- Then scratch a design into the surface with a pencil point, a fork, a knife, or a toothpick. Or make the design by pressing bottle caps, buttons, beads, or bits of jewelry into the clay.

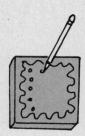

- Dry the tile in the oven, then paint. Coat the tile with clear nail polish when it is completely dry.

TO HANG YOUR TILE

- Paint the edges of a box-lid.
- Poke two holes at the top of the lid.
- Push strings through the holes and tie like this. →
- Glue the tile inside the lid. Wait until the glue is dry before you hang the tile.

PUZZLES

- Follow the directions for the tile, BUT . . .
- Before drying, cut the tile into six or eight uneven parts like this. →
- DO NOT separate the pieces.
- Bake the puzzle on foil in a 225° oven.
- Let the puzzle get cold. Then paint and decorate.
- Be sure to put on two coats of clear nail polish.
- Then scramble the pieces and put the puzzle together again.

Buttons, Pins, and

- Roll out a small slab of clay-dough.
- Use bottle tops and caps to cut out button shapes.
- Cut out other shapes (triangles, squares, hearts) with a nail file or butter knife.
- Dry in the air or in the oven.
- Paint and decorate. Cover both sides of the button or pin (front *and* back) with two or more coats of clear nail polish.
- After the nail polish dries, attach a small safety pin to the back of your clay-dough pin with white glue. Paste a small strip of tape across the safety pin to hold it in place like this. →

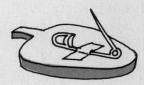

- Coat the tape with glue and let it dry before you wear your button or pin.

Pendants to Wear

· Roll out a slab of clay-dough.
· Use a nail file or butter knife to cut out any shape you wish. You can also use a small cookie cutter.

· Poke a rather large hole through the top of the shape like this. →

· Add tiny balls or coils of dough as decorations.
· Air or oven dry, then paint and decorate.
· Coat with at least two layers of clear nail polish.
· Hang on yarn or on a chain.

Holiday Ornaments

· Roll a slab of clay-dough.

· Cut out shapes with cookie
cutters, or cut shapes from
paper and put them on top of
the clay-dough slab. Then cut
around the shape with a butter
knife or nail file.
· Poke holes at the top of the
ornament for hanging.
· Dry, then paint and decorate.
· Cover with clear nail polish.

and Mobiles to Hang

- Hang ornaments and pendants on a mobile made of twigs and string. (See the picture.)
- Hang ornaments and pendants on their own little tree for a special holiday.
- Or hang them on a coat-hanger tree to make a wall decoration.

Stained-Glass Windows

You will need:
- Clay-dough for the frames.
- Hard candy such as lollipops, sour balls, or charms in assorted colors.
- Several paper bags.

Frames for the stained-glass windows can be made in two different ways. Do try them both:

FRAME 1

- Roll out a slab of clay-dough on foil.
- Cut out any shape you wish.
- Cut out openings inside the shape like this. →
- Poke a large hole at the top for hanging.

FRAME 2

- Draw a simple shape on foil with a felt pen.
- Roll very thin coils of clay-dough. Place the coils along the outline of the shape. Make sure all the coils are connected to each other.

- Dry frames in a 225° oven for 15 minutes.
- Take frames from the oven but leave them on the foil.
- Now turn the oven up to 375°.
- While the oven is heating, sort the hard candy. Put the red candy in one pile; the green candy in another; and so on.
- Put each pile of candy in a separate paper bag. To crush the candy, step on the bag or hit the bag with a hammer.
- Fill the openings in the frames with the crushed candy. Do not use more than one color in each opening.
- Bake the stained-glass windows for seven to nine minutes, or until the candy has melted.
- Wait until the windows are cold. Then peel off the foil.
- Decorate the frames if you wish.
- IMPORTANT: Cover the frames *and* the candy — front and back — with at least 2 coats of clear nail polish. This will keep the candy from dripping.
- Hang your stained-glass windows against the light.

Make Toys with Moving Parts

HERE ARE OTHER IDEAS FOR YOU TO TRY

CHECKERS

- Roll thick coils of clay-dough and slice them into checkers.
- Bake, paint, and decorate.

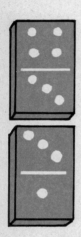

DOMINOES

- Cut thick slabs into oblongs that are the size of dominoes.
- Bake them in the oven.
- Paint the dominoes and let them dry.
- Mark the places for dots. Then paint them on. Coat with clear nail polish.

CANDLE HOLDER

- Flatten the bottom of a ball of clay-dough.
- Press your thumb into the center of the ball until the hole is large enough for a candle.
- Make designs on the sides. Add balls and coils or scratch the design into the dough.
- Bake, then paint and decorate.

SIGNS

- Shape clay-dough coils into letters of the alphabet. Make letters to spell out any words you wish.
- Bake and paint. When the letters are dry, glue them on cardboard.

SELF-PORTRAIT

- Make a figure of how you think you look.
- Make features by pulling dough out or adding pieces as needed.
- Bake, paint, and decorate.

DRY ALL TOYS IN A 225° OVEN.

CARS

- Roll a ball of clay-dough and model it into a car shape.
- Flatten four small balls of clay-dough for wheels. Poke a hole in the center of each wheel with a pencil.
- Push two toothpicks all the way through the sides of the car body to make axles.
- Dry the car parts in the oven.
- Paint on details. Put the wheels on the axles.

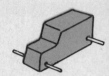

TRAINS

- Make a car shape with a long front end.
- Then add:
  - a coil for a smokestack;
  - a clay ball for a bell;
  - a clay ball for a headlight.
- Poke toothpicks in the sides for axles.
- Make four small wheels and two large wheels. Bake all parts. Put on wheels.

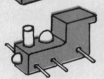

PEOPLE

- Roll an egg shape for a body. Add a small ball for the head.
- Poke two wire ties from plastic bags through shoulders and hips. Leave a long piece of wire on each side like this. →
- Flatten two coils for arms and two longer ones for legs. Poke holes through the tops. →
- Bake all parts. Paint a face on. Glue yarn on for hair.
- String the arms and legs on the wires. Turn the wire ends up to hold the arms and legs in place.

DOG

- Make an egg shape for the body. Add a small ball for the head.
- Add ears, tail, and nose. Push two wires through the body. →
- Flatten four coils for legs. Poke holes through the tops.
- Bake all parts. String legs on the wires. Turn wire ends up.